98

WHAT ON EARTH IS A
Sea Squirt

JENNY TESAR

 A B L A C K B I R C H P R E S S B O O K
WOODBRIDGE, CONNECTICUT

Published by Blackbirch Press, Inc.
One Bradley Road, Suite 104
Woodbridge, CT 06525

©1994 Blackbirch Press, Inc.
First Edition

Printed in Hong Kong

10 9 8 7 6 5 4 3 2 1

Photo Credits

Cover and title page: ©W. Gregory Brown/Animals Animals.
Pages 4—5: ©Patti Murray/Animals Animals; page 7: ©Clay H. Wiseman/Animals Animals; pages 8—9: ©G.I. Bernard/Animals Animals; page11: ©Bruce Watkins/Animals Animals; page 12: ©Mickey Gibson/Animals Animals; pages 14—15: ©G.I. Bernard/Animals Animals; page 16: ©David Hall/Photo Researchers, Inc.; page 17: ©Gregory G. Dimijian/Photo Researchers, Inc.; pages 4—5: ©Patti Murray/Animals Animals; pages 18—19: ©E.R. Degginger/Animals Animals; pages 20—21: ©David Hall/Photo Researchers, Inc.; pages 22—23: ©G.I. Bernard/Animals Animals; pages 24—25: ©Oxford Scientifc Films/Animals Animals; pages 26—27: ©Lourena Gould, Oxford Scientific Films/Animals Animals; page 28: ©Herb Segars/Animals Animals.

Library of Congress Cataloging-in-Publication Data
Tesar, Jenny E.
What on earth is a sea squirt? / Jenny Tesar. — 1st ed.
    p.   cm. — (What on earth series)
    Includes bibliographical references (p.   ) and index.
    ISBN 1-56711-091-6
    1. Sea Squirt—Juvenile literature.   [1. Sea squirt.   2. Ascidiacea.]
I. Title.   II. Series.
    1994
596.2—dc20   94-27858
                                                                          CIP
                                                                          AC

What does it look like?

Where does it live?

What does it eat?

How does it reproduce?

How does it survive?

TURN THESE PAGES AND FIND OUT!

A sea squirt looks like a little grape or vase. But it's actually an animal. It lives attached to rocks and other objects on the sea floor. When something disturbs a sea squirt, it squirts! Water shoots out of two openings near the top of the sea squirt's body.

A COLONY OF SEA SQUIRTS SWAYS WITH THE CURRENT IN THE PACIFIC WATERS OFF THE CALIFORNIA COAST.

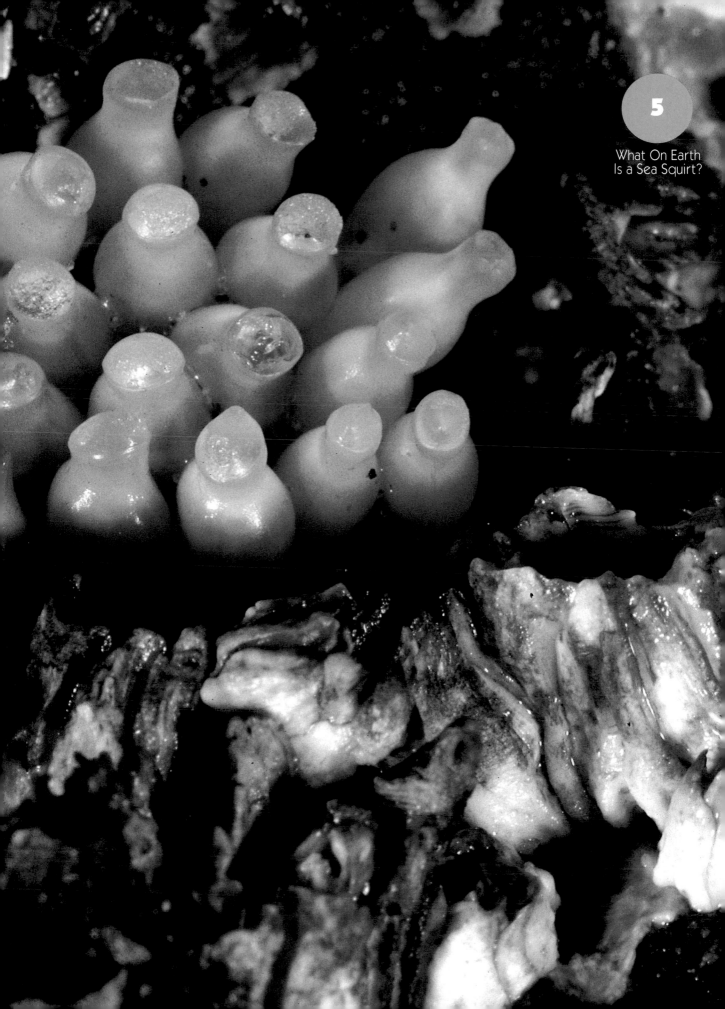

SEA SQUIRTS ARE
TUNICATES. TUNICATES
HAVE AN OUTER
COVERING CALLED A
TUNIC THAT PROTECTS
THEIR SOFT INSIDES.

Sea squirts belong to a group of animals called tunicates. These animals have an outer covering called a tunic. The tunic is like a coat. It protects the animal's soft insides. It also helps the sea squirt's body keep its shape.

There are two main groups of animals: vertebrates and invertebrates. Vertebrates have backbones. Invertebrates do not. Fish, birds, and humans are a few kinds of vertebrates. Insects, worms, and snails are examples of invertebrates.

Tunicates fall between the two groups. They do not have true backbones. But when they are young they have a structure that is like a backbone. It is a flexible rod-like structure called the notochord. Humans and other vertebrates have notochords too, but only before birth. By the time a vertebrate is born, its notochord has been replaced by a backbone.

IF YOU LOOK CLOSELY AT CERTAIN SEA SQUIRTS, YOU CAN SEE SOME OF THEIR ORGANS ON THE INSIDE.

There are three classes of tunicates: sea squirts, pyrosomas, and salps. Sea squirts belong to the Class Ascidiacea. This name comes from a Greek word that means "wineskin." A wineskin is a bag for holding wine. Traditionally, it is made from the skin of a goat or other animal.

Why did scientists give this name to sea squirts? The tunic of a sea squirt looks like a skin, or bag, that is filled with water. You have to look very closely at some sea squirts to see the stomach, heart, and other organs on the inside.

SEA SQUIRTS COME IN
A WIDE VARIETY OF
COLORS, FROM A DULL
GRAY TO BRIGHT
BLUES, ORANGES,
AND REDS.

There are hundreds of kinds, or species, of sea squirts. They come in many different colors, including green, gray, white, yellow, and bright red. Most sea squirts are less than one inch (3 centimeters) high. But some species are up to 8 inches (20 centimeters) high.

One end of a sea squirt's bag-like body is attached to a solid object on the sea floor. At the other end are two openings called siphons. Water enters the body through one siphon. Water leaves the body through the other siphon.

SEA SQUIRTS ATTACH THEMSELVES TO UNDERWATER OBJECTS AND OFTEN LIVE TOGETHER IN GROUPS CALLED COLONIES.

Sea squirts live attached to objects such as rocks, coral reefs, clam shells, wharf piles, ship bottoms, and underwater cables. Most species of sea squirts live in shallow water. Other species live thousands of feet below the ocean's surface.

Sea squirts can be found all over the world.

Many kinds of sea squirts live clustered together in clumps, or colonies. A colony may be large enough to form a colorful "carpet" on the surface of an underwater object.

A SEA SQUIRT FEEDS
BY TAKING IN WATER
THROUGH ONE SIPHON,
FILTERING IT, AND THEN
SENDING THE FILTERED
WATER OUT THROUGH
ITS OTHER SIPHON.

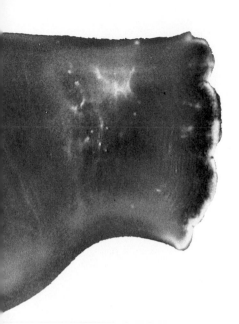

Sea squirts are filter feeders. That is, they feed on tiny food particles that they filter, or remove, from water. These food particles include bits of dead plants and animals.

Water constantly passes through a sea squirt's siphons. It flows through the incoming siphon into a large, basket-like "throat." Food particles in the water are trapped by sticky mucus on the walls of the throat. Then the water flows out of the body, through the outgoing siphon.

The food particles pass into the sea squirt's stomach and intestines. There, the food is digested and absorbed so it can later be used by all the cells of the body.

A LARGE, SINGLE SEA SQUIRT LIVES
INSIDE A COLORFUL BED OF CORAL.

Sea squirts share their ocean world with many other creatures. Sea squirts in tide pools live side-by-side with animals such as sea anemones and starfish. Sea squirts on ship bottoms live among mussels and barnacles.

Sea squirts often live attached to other living things. Many species grow on coral reefs. Some attach themselves to the roots of mangrove trees in coastal swamps. Others live on giant seaweeds in underwater "forests." Still others live on shells of mussels and clams. Some sea squirts even live on the bodies of larger sea squirts!

A COLONY OF PINK SEA SQUIRTS SHARES AN UNDERWATER REEF WITH ALGAE, SPONGES, CORALS, AND A BLACK-AND-WHITE CLOWN FISH.

Some fish eat sea squirts. Because a sea squirt lives attached to another object, it cannot run away from a fish. It depends on its tough tunic for protection. Certain kinds of sea squirts have muddy-colored tunics that blend well into the surroundings. This blending, called camouflage, hides the sea squirts from hungry fish.

SOME SEA SQUIRTS HAVE NO COLOR, WHICH ALLOWS THEM TO BETTER BLEND WITH THEIR SURROUNDINGS FOR PROTECTION.

19

SENSITIVE STRUCTURES ON THE INNER WALLS OF THE SIPHON HELP TO PREVENT LARGE PARTICLES FROM CLOGGING UP A SEA SQUIRT'S PASSAGEWAYS.

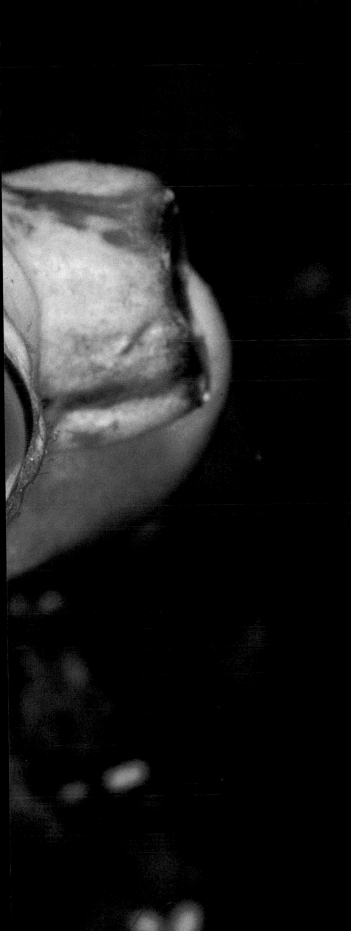

Sea squirts do not have sense organs such as eyes and ears. But they do have special cells that are very sensitive to touch. Some of these sensory cells are located in the inner walls of the siphons. They help to prevent large bits of matter from clogging up the throat and other parts of the body.

When a large particle enters the incoming siphon, the sea squirt's sensory cells quickly send messages to the muscles. The sea squirt's body then contracts. This forces water in the body to squirt out of both siphons. As the water shoots out, it carries the large particle out of the body and away from the sea squirt.

Most animals are either male or female. A sea squirt is both! It has both male and female reproductive organs. The male organs produce sperm. The female organs produce eggs. Usually, however, this does not happen at the same time. A sea squirt's eggs become ripe at one time. Its sperm ripen at another time.

Sea squirts release their eggs and sperm into the surrounding water. When an egg joins with a sperm, the egg is said to be fertilized. This fertilized egg will soon develop into a new sea squirt.

SEA SQUIRTS CONTAIN BOTH MALE AND FEMALE REPRODUCTIVE ORGANS. WHEN THEY ARE READY, EACH SEA SQUIRT RELEASES SPERM AND THEN EGGS INTO THE WATER.

The baby sea squirt that hatches from a fertilized egg does not look like its parents. It looks like the tadpole of a frog, though it is much, much smaller. It has a tiny tail, which it uses to swim around in the water.

After about a day, the young sea squirt settles to the ocean floor and attaches itself to a hard surface. Its body then begins to change into the adult form. The tail disappears and a tunic forms around the body.

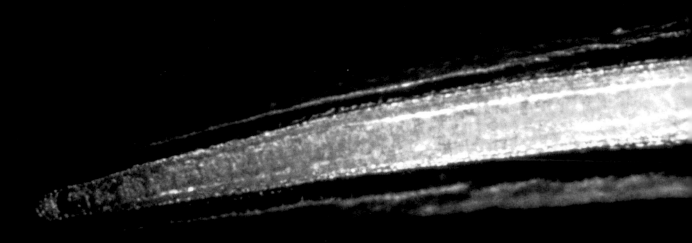

A NEWLY HATCHED SEA SQUIRT, WHICH CAN
SWIM, LOOKS VERY DIFFERENT FROM AN ADULT.

25

LARGE COLONIES OF SEA SQUIRTS ARE FORMED BY
BUDDING. THIS IS A PROCESS WHERE ONLY ONE
PARENT CREATES NEW SEA SQUIRTS.

A sea squirt colony may contain hundreds of
sea squirts. All the sea squirts in a colony form
through a reproductive process called budding.

In this process, small buds develop on the body
of a parent. These buds gradually grow into new
sea squirts.

SEA PEACHES, LIKE THIS
ONE, PROVIDE FOOD
FOR HUMANS IN
CERTAIN PARTS OF
THE WORLD.

29

What On Earth
Is a Sea Squirt?

Sea squirts are fascinating animals to study. Some studies of sea squirts have produced exciting information. One scientist discovered that sea squirts form kidney stones—just like humans do. Studying how sea squirts form and break down kidney stones may lead to treatments for people who have this problem with their kidneys.

Some sea squirts can be pests, especially when they cover boat bottoms and sewer pipes. Removing them from these surfaces is costly.

In some places, people eat sea squirts. In parts of Europe, people eat a species known as the sea peach. Its yellow-pinkish color and fuzzy-looking surface make it look like a real peach. But don't be fooled, the taste is very different!

Glossary

budding A process by which some sea squirts form buds on their body. The buds grow into new organisms, creating a colony.

camouflage Blending into the surroundings.

colony A group of animals of the same kind that live together.

digest Break down food particles so that they can be used by the body.

egg A female reproductive cell.

fertilization The joining of a male sex cell, called a sperm, and a female sex cell, called an egg. Fertilization is a part of reproduction.

filter feeder An animal, such as a sea squirt, that feeds on tiny particles. It removes, or filters, the particles from water flowing through part of its body.

mucus A sticky substance in a sea squirt's "throat" that traps food particles.

notochord A rod-like structure in young sea squirts. Before birth, vertebrates (animals with backbones) also have notochords.

reproduction Making more creatures of the same kind.

siphon A tube-like opening in a sea squirt, through which water enters or leaves the body.

species A group of living things that are closely related to one another. Members of a species can reproduce with one another. Sea peaches are a species. Blood-drop sea squirts are another species.

tunic The outer layer, or coat, of a sea squirt's body.

Further Reading

Carlisle, Madelyn W. *Let's Investigate Weird and Wonderful Sea Creatures*. Hauppauge, NY: Barron, 1993.

Carwardine, Mark. *Water Animals*. Ada, OK: Garrett Educational Corp. , 1989.

Coldrey, Jennifer. *Life in the Sea*. New York: Watts, 1989.

Downer, Ann. *Don't Blink Now! Capturing the Hidden World of Sea Creatures*. New York: Watts, 1991.

Kindersley, Dorling. *Sea Animals*. New York: Macmillan Child Group, 1992.

Rinard, Judy. *Amazing Animals of the Sea*. Washington, D.C.: National Geographic, 1981.

Wu, Norbert. *Exploring the World of the Kelp Forest*. San Francisco: Chronicle Books, 1992.

Index